# SOCCER JUDGE

# SOCCER JUDGE

## STAN LOVER

**MIRROR BOOKS**

First published in Great Britain
in August 1980 by Mirror Books Ltd.,
Athene House, 66/73 Shoe Lane,
London EC4P 4AB
for Mirror Group Newspapers Ltd.

Reproduced, printed and bound in Great Britain by
Cox & Wyman Ltd., Reading.

ISBN 0 85939 198 1

# CONTENTS

# Preface

The skills and thrills of modern football are often interlaced with incidents that interrupt the flow of the play. For example, during the World Cup 1978 each of the 38 matches played in Argentina was interrupted, on average, 115 times. In junior football the total can be nearer 200!

Many infringements are obvious. When the ball crosses the touch-line, or goal-line, the play is stopped automatically. We know that it will restart with a throw-in, a goal-kick, or a corner-kick; or with a kick-off when a goal is scored.

But in every match there are between 40 and 50 other stoppages for which the reasons are not so obvious. Free-kicks are awarded or play may be restarted with a dropped ball. Occasionally, players are disciplined for actions that do not appear to be serious. Basically, we do not understand what is happening. Some of the pleasure of the game is lost and we tend to question the officials in charge.

This book is intended, first, to check your current level of soccer knowledge and, second, to improve understanding of events during a soccer match in order to increase the enjoyment of playing or watching.

The 150 illustrated match problems are based on experience. Many may be seen several times in one match. In addition, there are descriptions and comments on classic examples of match problems famous in football history.

Soccer promotes friendship and endless discussion among its faithful followers. The illustrations here may be useful in highlighting points of debate on particular problems seen in recent matches.

With this book the reader can also achieve the status, among friends, of a soccer expert.

Stanley F. Lover

# Football match problems

## HOW MUCH DO YOU KNOW ABOUT FOOTBALL?

This book will tell you. It tests your knowledge of match play situations that are familiar but puzzling.

This is a book for every football fan. It will provoke endless discussion on actual match incidents and is an entertaining guide for the fan who wants to know more.

Each match problem has been compiled and illustrated by the author, who has had to solve these and other problems, as a soccer referee, in more than 1,000 matches at all levels of the game.

Stanley Lover is an internationally renowned expert in the teaching of the practical application of football law on the field of play.

Check your own rating as a SOCCER EXPERT with the guide included in the answers section. Your rating will improve as you restudy those questions which you have not answered correctly.

Use the illustrated problems to test your soccer friends and surprise them with your knowledge.

NOW, HOW MUCH DO YOU *REALLY* KNOW ABOUT FOOTBALL?

# MATCH
# PROBLEMS
# 1~20

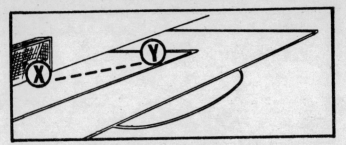

**1.** A free-kick is awarded to the defending team at X but the ball is kicked from Y. Is this allowed?

**2.** An attacker stands in an off-side position at a penalty-kick. The ball strikes a post. He runs in and scores. What is the correct decision?

**3.** When the match is started the ball is passed back to a team-mate. Is this allowed?

**4.** A goalkeeper shouts and distracts a team-mate in order to obtain the ball. Is this allowed?

**5.** The signal has been given for a free-kick. A defender runs to the ball and kicks it away. It goes to an attacker who scores. Is the goal allowed?

**6.** A player plays the ball with the top of his arm. Is this allowed?

**7.** At a corner-kick, an attacker and an opponent are 4 metres from the ball. Is this allowed?

**8.** A player decides to play without wearing boots. Is this allowed?

**9.** The end of the match is about to be signalled when a defender handles the ball inside the penalty-area. What is the correct action?

**10.** If a player jumps at the ball with both feet and an opponent is in possession, is this dangerous play?

**11.** An attacker heads the ball at the goal. It strikes the cross-bar, bounces behind the goal-line but spins back into play. Should a goal be awarded?

**12.** The ball is in play when a goalkeeper runs off the field to strike a spectator. What is the correct action?

**13.** An attacker is standing level with two defenders when the ball is passed to him by a colleague. There are no other players nearer to the goal-line. Is the attacker off-side?

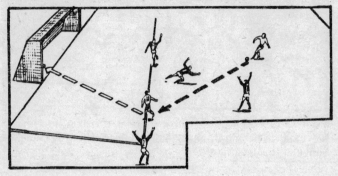

**14.** A defender makes no attempt to head the ball but intentionally backs into an opponent causing him to fall. What is the correct decision?

**15.** A goal is scored after 10 minutes' play. The referee realizes that the defending team has 12 players on the field. Which player must go off?

**16.** The ball is trapped between the legs of the goalkeeper. Is an opponent allowed to kick the ball?

**17.** At a kick-off the ball is kicked but before a team-mate can touch it, an opponent enters the centre circle. What action should be taken?

**18.** A player tries to distract an opponent at a throw-in by jumping up and down close to him. Is this allowed?

**19.** After a goal has been awarded, but before play has been restarted, a neutral linesman reports that the scorer punched the ball into the goal. Should the decision be changed?

**20.** A player charges an opponent in the back when the opponent is obstructing. Is this allowed?

# The mystery of the moving goalposts

Soccer's remarkable impact on the American sports public received a boost, in May 1976, when a major international tournament — the American Bicentennial Cup — was played in several important cities. The full national teams of Brazil, Italy, and England competed as a build-up to the 1978 World Cup. A fourth team representing the United States included international stars Pelé, Rodney Marsh and home-produced talent such as Bob Rigby and Kyle Rote Jun.

It was during the Team America match with England that a mysterious incident occurred. Bob Rigby, the US goalkeeper, was seen to be moving the goalposts while the ball was in his penalty area!

Goalposts are normally securely fixed into the ground but the goals at the John F. Kennedy Stadium, Philadelphia, were constructed as complete frameworks resting under their own weight on the soccer field. Although the posts were heavy, they were pushed about 1 metre behind the goal-line after a player had collided with a post. The incident was over in seconds but soccer fans who enjoy discussing match problems have posed the question, 'What would have been the correct action if the ball had entered the American goal before the posts were replaced?'

Soccer law does not insist that goalposts should be fixed to the ground — simply, '. . . placed on the centre of each goal-line . . .' In Philadelphia the posts were not in the correct position until Rigby pulled them to the goal-line. Therefore, in soccer law, a goal could not have been allowed.

If the referee was certain that the ball would have entered the goal a solution to this problem would have been to drop the ball near the goal-line at the feet of an attacker with an almost certain chance of scoring!

# MATCH
# PROBLEMS
# 21~40

**21.** An injured player receives permission to leave the field for treatment. Later he runs back onto the field, without permission, to kick the ball into goal. Is the goal allowed?

**22.** At half-time the team captains agree to restart the second half immediately but one player insists on an interval. What should the referee do now?

**23.** At a throw-in an attacker throws the ball direct into the opponents' goal. What is the correct decision?

**24.** When the ball is in play the referee notices that a goalkeeper changes places with a team-mate. What should he do?

**25.** From a penalty-kick the ball bursts on striking the goal-posts and rebounds into the field. What is the correct action?

**26.** A player deliberately holds up play by taking the ball to the corner-area and shielding it from opponents. Is this allowed?

**27.** A defender uses foul language to a linesman when he and the ball are inside his penalty-area. He is dismissed. How should play be restarted?

**28.** A player who is leaving the field, to be replaced by a substitute, strikes an opponent. Is the substitute allowed to take his place?

**29.** The ball is entering the goal but the goalkeeper pulls the crossbar down so that the ball sails over it. What is the correct action?

**30.** At a free-kick the signal is given. A defender then advances to 3 yards from the ball before it is kicked. Is this allowed?

**31.** A goalkeeper runs outside his penalty-area to head the ball. Is this allowed?

**32.** An attacker is in an off-side position but leaves the field to avoid interfering with play just before a team-mate scores. Is the goal allowed?

**33.** A defender kicks the ball towards the goalkeeper but it is intercepted by an attacker standing in an off-side position. He scores. Is the goal allowed?

**34.** An attacker has fallen inside the goal immediately before a team-mate kicks the ball into the goal. Is the goal allowed?

**35.** At a penalty-kick the signal is given but, before the ball is kicked, a player from each team runs into the penalty-area. The ball goes into the goal. What is the correct action?

**36.** A goalkeeper is seen to be scraping a line from the centre of his goal to the goal-area line. Is this allowed?

**37.** Are players allowed to smoke during a match?

**38.** Play is stopped when a player is seriously injured. A defender then strikes an opponent inside the penalty-area. He is dismissed. How should the play be restarted?

**39**. From a goal-kick the ball is returned to the goalkeeper when it reaches the penalty-area boundary line. Is this allowed?

**40.** At the end of a defensive wall a defender extends his arm. The ball strikes it and ricochets over the crossbar. What is the correct decision?

# Leeds~champions but for 'off-side' goal?

During the 1970s one of the most discussed problems concerned an 'off-side' goal which Leeds United supporters believe cost their favourite team the First Division Championship of the Football League.

Leeds were well placed to become champions when West Bromwich Albion visited Elland Road at the end of the 1971 season. Leeds lost 1—2, but the manner in which the game was decided provoked intense publicity and television debate. West Bromwich were allowed a goal that was strongly contested by the Leeds players, who claimed that an opponent was off-side at the time.

The incident is illustrated in the diagram opposite. On the right, player No.6 (Hunter of Leeds) is in possession of the ball just inside the opponents' half. He attempts to pass the ball to a colleague. The pass is bad and the ball strikes opponent No.8 (Brown). At this moment opponent No.10 (Suggett) is in an off-side position in the Leeds half. After striking Brown, the ball rebounds towards the Leeds half and Brown follows it.

The linesman signals Suggett's off-side position but the referee (Mr R. Tinkler) waves play on. Brown runs on into the Leeds penalty-area and passes the ball to his No.9 (Astle), who scores. Leeds protest, claiming that, when the ball rebounded from Brown, Suggett was interfering with the play. But the referee was well placed to judge the situation and decided that there was no pass intended by Brown towards Suggett, so that Suggett was not involved in the next phase of play.

The goal was allowed and Leeds ended the season in second place behind Arsenal. The margin was one point.

This incident highlights two basic points of the off-side law. The first is a matter of fact. Suggett was in an off-side position. The second is a matter of opinion. Was he interfering with play or trying to gain an advantage? In the opinion of the Leeds players, Suggett was guilty, but the referee thought otherwise and, in soccer law, it is his opinion that counts.

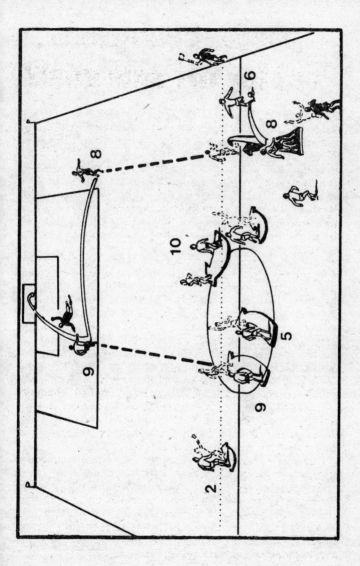

# MATCH
# PROBLEMS
# 41~60

**41.** During a competition match the crossbar is broken and cannot be repaired. Can a rope be used in place of the crossbar?

**42.** A player attempts to kick an opponent but he does not make contact. Is this an offence?

**43.** An attacker is in an off-side position when he receives the ball from a throw-in. He scores. Is the goal allowed?

**44.** A defender commits two offences at the same time by obstructing an opponent and handling the ball. What is the correct decision?

**45.** The referee signals a goal but he then realizes that the ball has not crossed the goal-line. Should he change his decision?

**46.** A player pretends to play the ball but deliberately makes contact with his opponent's leg over the top of the ball. Is this dangerous play?

**47.** A throw-in is taken from the correct position but the ball enters the field several metres from the thrower. What is the correct action?

**48.** The captain who has won the toss wants to keep the ball for the kick-off. Is this allowed?

**49.** At a goal-kick the goalkeeper kicks the ball directly to a colleague who is in an off-side position in the opponents' half. Is he off-side?

**50.** Playing time is extended for a penalty-kick. The goalkeeper deflects the ball onto a post. It rebounds to the kicker and he scores. Is the goal allowed?

**51.** An attacker jumps to head the ball inside the penalty-area. A defender ignores the ball and jumps at the attacker. What is the correct decision?

**52.** From a kick-off the ball is kicked directly into the opponents' goal. What is the correct decision?

**53.** A defender, standing outside the penalty-area, handles the ball when it is on the penalty-area boundary line. What is the correct decision?

**54.** A defender and an opponent have run over the goal-line. The defender prevents the opponent from going back onto the field of play when the ball is in the penalty-area. What action is called for?

**55.** A player is injured and leaves the field for treatment. His captain wants to replace him with a substitute until he is fit to play again. Is this in order?

**56.** Aided by a strong wind a goalkeeper throws the ball from his penalty-area into the opponents' goal. Is the goal allowed?

**57.** From a direct free-kick the ball strikes the referee and is deflected into the goal. What is the correct decision?

**58.** At a penalty-kick the ball strikes the crossbar and returns to the kicker. He kicks the ball into the goal. Is the goal allowed?

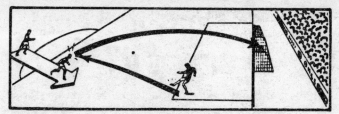

**59.** After the ball is kicked from a goal-kick an attacker runs into the penalty-area and heads the ball into the goal. Is the goal allowed?

**60.** A defender attempts to kick the ball when it is close to the head of an opponent. Is this allowed?

# World Cup Final goal- or was it?

Tension and drama are basic ingredients in any exciting soccer match. These were certainly present during the World Cup Final of 1966 when England played West Germany at Wembley in front of 97,000 spectators. Many millions watched the match on television.

England held a winning lead of 2—1 with only seconds to play. Home supporters were already cheering a great victory when the Germans equalized. From a free-kick Weber slid the ball beyond the reach of England's goalkeeper Gordon Banks. The exhausted players faced 30 agonizing minutes of extra time. For the Germans it meant another chance to snatch the prize; for the English — a victory to be won again.

Towards the end of the first period of extra time an incident occurred that sealed the fate of this emotional and thrilling match. The incident was highly dramatic at the time and has been debated ever since. Alan Ball, England's compact but nonstop midfield player, centred the ball from the right touch-line to Geoff Hurst. Hurst controlled the ball then turned and crashed it towards the German goal. As illustrated opposite, the ball struck the underside of the crossbar and was deflected down to the goal-line. From there it bounced to Weber who headed it to safety.

The Swiss referee, Gottfried Dienst, was uncertain whether the ball had bounced on or behind the goal-line and looked anxiously towards his Russian linesman, Tofik Bakhramov. The linesman's flag was raised. The play was stopped and millions held their breath as the referee ran to the touchline for an animated consultation. He turned and pointed to the centre of the field — a goal. Or was it? Was the *whole* of the ball behind the goal-line when it touched the ground?

The English were happy with the decision, the Germans protested but to no avail. The score was 3—2. In the last seconds of extra time Hurst scored his third and England's fourth goal: result 4—2.

What would have been the fate of the match if England's third goal had been disallowed? Exhaustive studies of photographs and films have not proved conclusively that the ball did cross the goal-line.

The question mark remains in football history but the result will never be changed because, as soccer law states, the referee's decision is final.

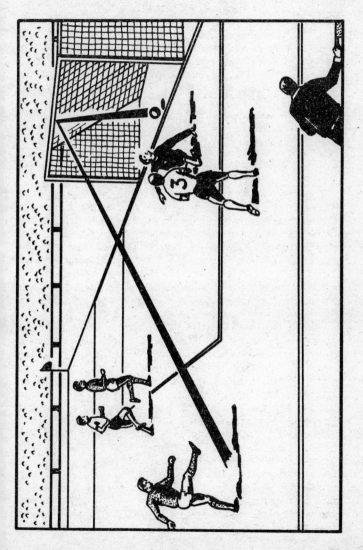

# MATCH
# PROBLEMS
# 61~80

**61.** Play continues while a player on the field receives treatment from a trainer who is outside the touchline. Is this allowed?

**62.** After catching the ball the goalkeeper falls inside the arc which is added to the penalty-area. What is the correct decision?

**63.** An attacker runs over the touchline to avoid an opponent. He is tripped by a substitute. What is the correct action?

**64.** A goalkeeper runs 8 paces bouncing the ball on the ground between his hands. Is there a problem here?

**65.** After a free-kick is taken, defenders rush forward leaving an attacker in an off-side position. He scores. Is the goal allowed?

**66.** A player charges an opponent in the chest. Is this allowed?

**67.** From the kick-off the ball goes forward but swerves back behind the centre-line before it is touched by another player. What is the correct action?

**68.** The referee is knocked unconscious by the ball which then goes into the goal. Is the goal allowed?

**69.** A player charges an opponent fairly when the ball is at a distance of 6 yards. Is this allowed?

**70.** An attacker traps the ball between his face and his shoulder and runs into the opposing goal. Is the goal allowed?

**71.** An attacker, No.9, has been declared off-side but, before the free-kick is taken, he is pushed by a defender inside the penalty-area. What is the correct action?

**72.** An attacker is in a good position to score inside the penalty-area when he is pulled back by an opponent who grabs the attacker's hair. What is the correct action?

**73.** From a corner-kick the ball goes directly into the goal before it is touched by a player. Is the goal allowed?

**74.** The match is finished. A player then strikes an opponent. Can any action be taken now?

**75.** A defender attempts to stop the ball with his hand but deflects it into the goal. Is it a goal or a penalty-kick?

**76.** An attacker is about to score when he is brought down by a rugby tackle inside the penalty-area. What action must be taken?

**77.** A player swears who is inside the field and abuses his own trainer when the ball is in play. Can any action be taken?

**78.** An attacker is tripped in the penalty-area but, before the whistle is blown, he kicks the ball into the goal. Is it a goal or a penalty-kick?

**79.** A goalkeeper catches the ball in front of the goal-line but his body is behind the goal-line. What is the correct decision?

**80.** A defender obstructs an opponent by holding his shirt. What is the correct decision?

# The 'Donkey-kick' - is it legal?

The sight of defenders in the form of a line, or wall, in front of a free-kick is an accepted part of modern football. The tactic is not forbidden in soccer law providing the defenders are 10 yards (9.15 metres) from the ball.

To counter the defensive wall, attacking players devise various moves intended to deceive their opponents. Some are simple, others have a touch of genius in their design. One controversial tactic, which was eventually referred to soccer's law authority, the International FA Board, was introduced by Coventry City players in 1971. It was named the 'donkey-kick'. It was simple and successful, but was it fair?

Coventry were awarded an indirect free-kick near their opponents' penalty-area. While defenders were busy forming a wall, two Coventry players put into effect the carefully rehearsed 'donkey-kick'. The ball was in the correct position for the free-kick as Willie Carr walked slowly towards it. He appeared to step over the ball but stopped. Then he gripped the ball between his heels and kicked both feet up behind, like the action of a donkey. (See facing illustration.)

Hunt, standing casually a few metres away, suddenly ran forward and crashed the ball into the net with a brilliant volley. Was it a goal? Yes, said Mr Dawes, the referee. After the match a film of the incident was screened before millions of TV soccer fans. The debate that followed questioned the validity of the tactic. Was the 'donkey-kick' a legal kick at the ball?

In June 1971 the International FA Board ruled that, '. . . the ball was not kicked in the accepted sense of the word'. As a result, it was illegal, and the free-kick should have been retaken. But the ruling came months after the incident and the goal was not cancelled.

Many officials agreed that, faced with the 'donkey-kick' for the first time, they would have made the same decision as Mr Dawes. Now we know it is not acceptable.

What new surprises lie in store for us to cause as much controversy as the 'donkey-kick'? Who knows — you may see it in the next match you watch!

# MATCH
# PROBLEMS
# 81~100

**81.** A defender uses the shoulders of a team-mate to gain height in heading the ball. Is this allowed?

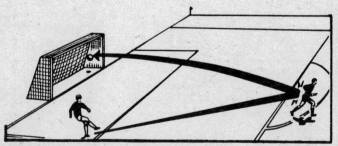

**82.** From a goal-kick the ball passes outside the penalty-area, strikes the referee, and rebounds into the goal. What is the correct decision?

**83.** Two players of the same team are fighting inside their penalty-area. Play is stopped and the players are dismissed. How should the play be restarted?

**84.** The ball is going towards the goal-line for a goal-kick. A defender shields it from an opponent without attempting to play it. Is this allowed?

**85.** The signal has been given for a penalty-kick but, before the ball is kicked, the goalkeeper runs from his goal. Should the kick be delayed?

**86.** From a throw-in a defender throws the ball back to his goalkeeper but it goes directly into the goal. What is the correct decision?

**87.** An attacker charges the goalkeeper fairly when the goal-keeper is holding the ball inside the goal-area. Is this allowed?

**88.** An attacker is in an off-side position when the ball is passed to him by a team-mate, but he runs back into his own half before playing the ball. Is he off-side?

**89.** Before the start of a match a team captain objects to the wearing of track-suit trousers by the opponents' goalkeeper. What action should be taken?

**90.** An indirect free-kick is to be taken nearer than 9.15m (10 yards) from the goal. Defenders line up on the goal-line between and outside the goalposts. Is this allowed?

**91.** Play is restarted by dropping the ball. The ball falls to an attacker in an off-side position. He scores. What is the correct decision?

**92.** A defender forces an opponent to change direction by stretching his arms and moving from side to side. Is this allowed?

**93.** When taking a penalty-kick a player passes his foot over the ball (1), causing the goalkeeper to move, then he scores (2). Is the goal allowed?

**94.** An injured player wants to come back onto the field after treatment. Must he wait for a normal stoppage of play?

**95.** From a corner-kick the ball goes to an attacker who has only one defender between himself and the goal-line. He scores. Is it a goal or a free-kick for off-side?

**96.** Before play starts a player strikes an opponent and is dismissed. Can another player take his place?

**97.** A player who is wearing a captain's armband protests against a decision. Is this allowed?

**98.** After the ball is passed forward an attacker runs from his own half into an off-side position. He kicks the ball into the goal. Is the goal allowed?

**99.** From a penalty-kick the ball is passed back to another attacker who runs into the penalty-area and scores. Is the goal allowed?

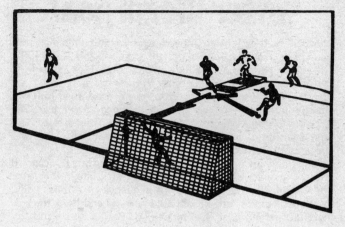

**100.** When No.12 scores a goal, the referee realizes that he is a substitute who has replaced a team-mate at half-time without notifying the referee. Is the goal allowed?

# Relegation~
# after illegal goal

Football facts are often interesting but limited in narrative value. For example, it is a fact that, on the 2nd April 1952, Tottenham Hotspur beat Huddersfield Town 1—0 in the First Division of the Football League. But behind that fact lies a story which is recorded in soccer history because the result was directly influenced by an error in applying soccer law. The error could also have changed Huddersfield Town's status as a First Division club. A few days after the match the club was relegated to the Second Division.

The incident, which caused much controversy, occurred after Tottenham were awarded a corner-kick late in the game. The facing illustration shows the sequence of events. Baily, the Spurs outside left, kicked a corner low and hard towards the Huddersfield goal. The referee, Mr Barnes, was struck by the ball and dazed for a few seconds. The next thing he saw was the ball being headed into the goal by Duquemin, the Spurs centre-forward. He immediately awarded a goal and was surprised by the protests of the Huddersfield players.

The protests were not unreasonable. What Mr Barnes had not seen was that the ball had rebounded off himself to Baily, and that Baily had kicked the ball again before Duquemin scored. Soccer law does not allow a player who takes a corner-kick to play the ball again until it has been touched by another player. The fact that the ball rebounded from the referee makes no difference. Mr Barnes discussed the problem with a linesman but found no reason to cancel the goal.

After the match Huddersfield filed a formal protest with the Football League requesting that the match be declared invalid and asking for it to be replayed. The League rejected the protest as did a special appeals court some weeks later. As a result, Huddersfield were denied another chance of avoiding relegation.

This problem was a classic case of the referee's being right even when he was wrong!

The story has a happy sequel — Huddersfield were promoted back to the First Division at the end of the following season.

# MATCH PROBLEMS 101-120

**101**. The ball is in play in the centre of the field when the referee sees a defender, standing in his own penalty-area, push an opponent. Where is the ball placed for the free-kick?

**102**. A goalkeeper falls on the ball and makes no attempt to release it. Is this allowed.

**103.** A player disobeys a team instruction and is dismissed by his captain. Is this allowed?

**104.** At a corner-kick the ball swerves over the goal-line but back into play. Should the match continue?

**105.** A goalkeeper throws the ball over an opponent's head and catches it after taking 6 steps. Is this allowed?

**106.** The ball is kicked hard and strikes the hand of a defender in the penalty-area. Should the referee award a penalty?

**107.** When trying to punch the ball a goalkeeper accidentally strikes an opponent. Should a free-kick be awarded?

**108.** At a corner-kick the goalkeeper intentionally obstructs an opponent with his arm. Is the award an indirect free-kick or a penalty?

**109.** A player refuses to remove religious objects from his person which the referee considers to be dangerous to other players. What should be done now?

**110.** In a tackle from behind a player misses the ball and trips an opponent. What is the decision?

**111.** When the ball is dropped to restart play, it touches the foot of a player before bouncing, and crosses the touchline. What is the correct action?

**112.** Before a throw-in is taken a player kicks an opponent. What action should be taken and how is play restarted?

**113.** A substitute does not wear the same coloured shirt as his team-mates. Does this matter?

**114.** A defender moves over his goal-line to leave an attacker in an off-side position. The ball goes into the goal. Is the goal allowed?

**115.** What is the correct pressure of the ball before the start of play?

**116.** When the ball is kicked into the penalty-area the goalkeeper shouts at an opponent to distract him. What action can be taken?

**117.** A player is given permission to leave the field (1). Before he can do so, he receives a pass (2), and scores (3). Is the goal allowed?

**118.** Is an attacker allowed to stand on the opponents' goal-line when a free-kick has been awarded to the defending team outside the penalty-area?

**119.** From a corner-kick the ball strikes a goalpost and returns to the kicker. He passes the ball to a team-mate who scores. Is the goal allowed?

**120.** The ball is kicked towards an attacker, who is in an off-side position near the goal, but it strikes a defender and is deflected to the attacker, who scores. Is the goal allowed?

# Witchcraft in soccer

According to some travellers' tales, Africa is a dark continent full of mystery. Some of these mysteries find their way onto the soccer field. It is a fact that the African soccer follower is as fanatical about his favourite team as is his European or South American counterpart. Dances and chants of African supporters are remarkably similar to those performed in other soccer continents. African football also has a special ingredient — witchcraft, which calls upon powerful forces to influence the fortunes of teams and individual players. These forces are described as *muti* or medicine. Medicine can be good or bad, according to who is giving or receiving it, as the following true stories show:

Some supporters carry a rabbit's foot, or a goat's foot, wrapped in cloth containing special herbs and meaty substances, to keep away evil spirits from their team. Talismans of this kind are often found near a soccer field after a big match.

A team may refuse to play with a ball that has been touched by the manager of the opposing team because he may have put a magic spell on it to favour his own team.

A goalkeeper who throws his cap into the back of his goal may be considered to have put a spell on the goal to prevent the opposing team from scoring.

When the ball is kicked into the crowd it may quite easily be knifed by a fan of the losing side to kill evil spirits.

At one match the teams were ready for the kick-off when a spectator rushed on to the centre of the field and placed an object under the ball. Knowing that the teams would not start until the 'spell' had been removed, the referee chased and caught the offender. He led him back to the ball and ordered the players to stand well clear while the fan lifted it to expose the dark secret — the top of a Coca-Cola bottle!

Africans are not alone in believing in witchcraft or superstitions to help their cause. Many players, in Europe and other continents, have special charms for good luck, or follow certain habits such as touching or seeing a 'lucky' object, or person, wearing 'lucky' boots, colours, numbers, etc.

In order to solve match problems involving witchcraft, special knowledge and diplomacy are called for.

# MATCH
# PROBLEMS
# 121~140

**121.** A player, who is being cautioned, stubbornly refuses to provide the referee with his name. What should the referee do now?

**122.** The ball is prevented from entering the goal by the goal-keeper's crash helmet, which he has placed beside the goalpost. Should a goal be awarded?

**123.** A team coach shouts instructions to his players during the match. Is this allowed?

**124.** A goalkeeper is attempting to kick the ball when he is challenged by an opponent who steps in front of him. Is this allowed?

**125.** After 10 minutes' play the referee realizes that two players of the same team are wearing the same number. Which player should be dismissed?

**126.** When a penalty-kick is awarded the attacking team's goal-keeper says that he will take the kick. Is this allowed?

**127.** A linesman signals the ball out of play for a goal-kick but, before the whistle is sounded, a defender kicks an opponent inside the penalty-area. What is the correct decision?

**128.** For a competition match the referee declares the field unplayable but the two team managers insist that the match be played. What happens now?

**129** At a throw-in a player has one foot off the ground when the ball is thrown. Is there a problem here?

**130.** An attacker fairly charges a goalkeeper when the ball is within playing distance inside the goal-area. Is this allowed?

**131.** A player removes a corner-post to obtain more space before taking a corner-kick. Is this allowed?

**132.** The goalkeeper catches the ball. An attacker attempts to block the kick by raising his foot, as shown. Is this allowed?

**133.** At a goal-kick, an attacker enters the penalty-area before the ball has left the area. He is then pushed by a defender. What is the correct action?

**134.** From a free-kick, outside the penalty-area, a defender passes the ball back to his goalkeeper. The goalkeeper does not touch the ball before it goes into the goal. What is the correct action?

**135.** A free-kick has been awarded for obstruction by a defender. The ball is kicked directly into the goal. Is the goal allowed?

**136.** A goalkeeper pushes an opponent with the ball inside the penalty-area. What is the correct decision?

**137.** Taking a free-kick inside his penalty-area, a defender passes the ball to his goalkeeper but it goes into the goal. Is the goal allowed?

**138.** A player attempts to kick the ball when it is 1 metre above the ground and an opponent is trying to head it. Which player should be penalized?

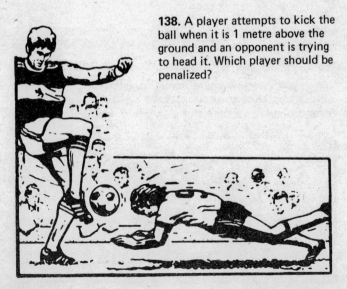

**139.** A substitute stands behind the goal-line and shouts to distract the opponents' goalkeeper. Can action be taken?

**140.** At a free-kick defenders form a line 9.15 metres (10 yards) from the ball. Three attackers then line up between the defenders and the ball. Is this allowed?

# One shot ~ three months in prison

Soccer match problems are not always created by the players. Take the case of Jean-Marc Luccheti, a fanatical supporter of the Corsican team Calenzana.

The 23rd April 1978 was an important date for Jean-Marc. Calenzana were playing a vital relegation match against their big rivals from Murato, near Bastia. Towards the end of a tense game Calenzana were holding Murato to a draw to gain a valuable point. Suddenly, a Murato forward ran through the defence and kicked the ball towards an empty goal.

Jean-Marc, standing on the touch-line, had given his team his usual vocal encouragement but, was it enough? The ball was surely going into the goal. It would be a catastrophe if Murato scored now.

He decided that he would have to do something decisive. He swiftly produced a gun from his pocket and fired at the ball. His aim was true. The ball instantly dropped, with a final rush of air from its lifeless carcase, just short of the goal-line.

Jean-Marc must have known that soccer law does not allow a goal to be scored if interference from an 'outside agent' prevents the ball from entering the goal. In the confusion that followed, the match was ended by the referee who declared that he had neither seen nor heard anything unusual!

Calenzana had escaped defeat but Jean-Marc was arrested and had to pay the price for his loyalty. For possessing an illegal weapon he was sentenced to three months in prison.

# MATCH
# PROBLEMS
# 141~150

**141.** At a corner-kick an attacker positions himself in front of the goalkeeper. Is this allowed?

**142.** The goalkeeper, inside his penalty-area, throws the ball violently at an opponent who is outside the area. What is the correct decision?

**143.** The referee has stopped play 2 minutes too soon at half-time and the players are leaving the field. Should he recall the players or add 2 minutes to the second half?

**144.** A player can only take a throw-in with one arm because the other is injured. Is this allowed?

**145.** A player is dismissed. Three other players are abusive and are also dismissed leaving only 7 players in one team. Should the match continue?

**146.** A player plays the ball with a sliding tackle. An opponent falls over the tackler's leg. What action should be taken?

**147.** Before a penalty-kick is taken a defender obtains permission to leave the field. He then stands beside a goalpost behind the goal-line. Is this allowed?

**148.** From a goal-kick the ball swerves over the goal-line before reaching the penalty-area boundary line. What is the correct decision?

**149.** An attacker is unable to avoid the ball when it is kicked onto his arm. It bounces kindly for him and he scores. Should the goal be allowed?

**150.** From a free-kick a player lifts the ball in one movement over a defensive wall. Is this allowed?

# ANSWERS

**1.** Yes. A change of law in 1978 allows the defending team this advantage.

**2.** An indirect free-kick must be awarded for off-side.

**3.** No. The kick-off must be retaken because the ball has not been kicked forward.

**4.** Yes. Tactical calling to team-mates is allowed but not if it is intended to distract an opponent.

**5.** No. The free-kick must be taken by an attacker. The defender should be cautioned.

**6.** No. The whole of the arm is included in the term, 'handling of the ball'. A direct free-kick is the correct punishment, or a penalty-kick if the infringement took place inside the offender's penalty-area.

**7.** No. The opposing player must be at least 9.15 metres (10 yards) from the ball.

**8.** Yes, but not in competition matches when most of the other players are wearing boots or shoes.

**9.** A penalty-kick must be awarded and completed before ending the match.

**10.** Not unless there is any *real* danger to the opponent.

**11.** Yes, because the ball has crossed the goal-line.

**12.** Dismiss the goalkeeper. Play is restarted with an indirect free-kick for leaving the field without permission.

**13.** Yes, because he does not have two or more opponents *between* himself and the goal-line.

**14.** The offence is tripping an opponent with the body. A direct free-kick should be awarded, or a penalty-kick if the offence took place inside the penalty-area.

**15** All players must leave and a new match started with the correct number of players.

**16.** No. This is dangerous play. An indirect free-kick should be awarded against the opponent.

**17.** None. The ball is in play. It is not necessary for two attackers to touch it before opponents enter the centre-circle.

**18.** No. The player should be cautioned for ungentlemanly conduct.

**19.** Yes. A direct free-kick awarded to the defending team, because their opponents handled the ball, is the correct decision.

**20.** No. A charge in the back is very dangerous. A direct free-kick is the correct award, or a penalty-kick if the offence was committed by a defender inside his own penalty-area.

**21.** No. The player must be cautioned for coming back onto the field without permission, and the goal disallowed. An indirect free-kick is awarded.

**22.** Grant an interval because all players have a right to an interval. The referee has no power to refuse.

**23.** A goal cannot be scored direct from a throw-in. The correct decision is a goal-kick.

**24.** Wait for a normal stoppage of play, then caution both players because the referee must be informed before such an exchange takes place.

**25.** The game must be stopped and then restarted by dropping another ball near the goalposts.

**26.** Yes. The ball is in play and this is a legitimate tactic.

**27.** An indirect free-kick should be awarded to the opposing team where the defender was when he committed the offence.

**28.** No. The offending player is dismissed and cannot be replaced.

**29.** A goal cannot be allowed but the goalkeeper should be cautioned for ungentlemanly conduct and an indirect free-kick awarded to the opponents.

**30.** No. Defending players must remain at least 9.15 metres (10 yards) from the ball until it is kicked into play.

**31.** Yes. But he must not touch the ball with his hands outside the penalty-area.

**32.** Yes. As shown, the attacker is clearly avoiding the play and should not be penalized.

**33.** Yes, because the attacker has received the ball direct from an opponent.

**34.** Yes. As shown the attacker is making no attempt to interfere with play or with an opponent.

**35.** The goal is not allowed. Law 14 requires the referee to caution the two players. The penalty-kick must then be retaken.

**36.** No. The goalkeeper should be cautioned. The mark is an artificial aid to skill.

**37.** No. The referee is required to caution the player for an act of ungentlemanly conduct.

**38.** Play is restarted with a dropped ball where the ball was when the match was stopped because the offence occurred when the ball was not in play.

**39.** No. The ball must pass completely outside the penalty-area before it can be played. The goal-kick must be retaken.

**40.** The defender has intentionally allowed the ball to strike his arm. A direct free-kick (or a penalty-kick if inside the penalty-area) should be awarded.

**41.** No, not in a competition match. The match must be abandoned.

**42.** Attempting to kick an opponent is as serious as actually kicking him. A direct free-kick is the correct decision unless the offence took place inside the offender's penalty-area, in which case a penalty-kick is awarded.

**43.** Yes, a player cannot be off-side from a throw-in.

**44.** Handling the ball is the more serious offence. A direct free-kick is the correct award, or a penalty-kick if the offence took place inside the offender's penalty-area.

**45.** Yes. Play should be restarted by dropping the ball.

**46.** No. It is serious foul play for which the offender should be dismissed and a direct free-kick awarded or a penalty-kick if inside his penalty-area.

**47.** The throw-in must be retaken.

**48.** Yes. He may choose the direction of play or the kick-off.

**49.** A player cannot be off-side from a goal-kick.

**50.** No. The match is considered to be terminated when the ball rebounds into play.

**51.** A penalty-kick for jumping at an opponent.

**52.** A goal-kick, because a goal cannot be scored direct from a kick-off.

**53.** A penalty-kick because the boundary line is included in the penalty-area.

**54.** Play must be stopped and the defender cautioned. Play must be restarted with a dropped ball because the offence occurred outside the field of play.

**55.** No. A player who has been replaced is not allowed to play again in the match.

**56.** Yes. Law 10 confirms that the goalkeeper may score in this manner.

**57.** A goal and a black mark to the referee for bad positioning!

**58.** No. The penalty-kicker has played the ball twice before another player has touched it. The correct decision is an indirect free-kick.

**59.** No. The ball is not in play until it passes outside the penalty-area. The goal-kick must be retaken.

**60.** No. This is dangerous play. An indirect free-kick is the correct decision.

**61.** No. The player must obtain permission to leave the field for treatment.

**62.** A direct free-kick is awarded against the goalkeeper for handling the ball outside the penalty-area.

**63.** Play must be stopped and the substitute cautioned. Play is restarted with a dropped ball.

**64.** Yes. The goalkeeper is allowed a maximum of 4 paces when bouncing the ball. An indirect free-kick is the correct award.

**65.** Yes, because the attacker was not off-side when the ball was kicked into play.

**66.** No. The correct award is a direct free-kick for charging in a dangerous manner, or a penalty-kick if the offender was inside his own penalty-area.

**67.** Play should continue because the ball was in play when it was kicked forward into the other half.

**68.** Yes, if, in the opinion of a neutral linesman, the goal was properly scored.

**69.** No. Although the charge is fair the ball is not within playing distance, i.e., about 2-3 yards. An indirect free-kick is the correct decision.

**70.** No. The player should be cautioned and an indirect free-kick awarded. This is regarded as ungentlemanly conduct.

**71.** The defender should be cautioned and play restarted with a free-kick to his team (for the off-side offence).

**72.** The opponent should be dismissed for serious foul play, and a penalty-kick awarded to the attacking team.

**73.** Yes. A goal can be scored direct from a corner-kick.

**74.** Yes. The offending player must be reported as if the incident had occurred during play.

**75.** A goal. The referee is allowed to apply 'advantage' in this case.

**76.** The offending player should be dismissed for serious foul play. A penalty-kick must also be awarded.

**77.** Yes. The player should be dismissed and the match restarted with an indirect free-kick.

**78.** A goal should be awarded by applying the 'advantage' clause of Law 5.

**79.** Play should continue because the ball has not crossed the goal-line.

**80.** A direct free-kick for holding an opponent, or a penalty-kick if inside the penalty-area. The defender may also be cautioned for ungentlemanly conduct.

**81.** No. The game should be stopped, the defender cautioned and an indirect free-kick awarded.

**82.** A corner-kick must be awarded.

**83.** Play should be restarted with an indirect free-kick.

**84.** Yes, because the ball is within playing distance of the defender.

**85.** No, but if a goal is not scored the penalty-kick must be retaken.

**86.** A corner-kick must be awarded.

**87.** Yes. The goalkeeper may also be charged if he is obstructing an opponent.

**88.** Yes. The attacker was off-side at the moment the ball was played.

**89.** No action, because any player may wear track-suit trousers or similar trousers.

**90.** No. All defenders must be on the goal-line and between, not outside, the goal-posts.

**91.** A goal. A player cannot be off-side from a dropped ball.

**92.** No. The defender must be cautioned and an indirect free-kick awarded.

**93.** No. The penalty-kicker should be cautioned for ungentlemanly conduct. The penalty-kick must be retaken.

**94.** No. He may rejoin during play but only after receiving a signal from the referee.

**95.** A goal is correct. A player cannot be off-side from a corner-kick.

**96.** Yes, because the match had not started.

**97.** No. A team captain is not allowed to question the decision of a referee. He should be cautioned for showing dissent.

**98.** Yes, because the attacker was in his own half when the ball was passed forward.

**99.** No, because the ball must be kicked forward from the penalty-kick. The kick must be retaken.

**100.** Yes, but the substitute must be cautioned.

**101.** On the penalty-mark because the offence occurred in the penalty-area, which means a penalty-kick.

**102.** No. The goalkeeper is wasting time. An indirect free-kick should be awarded.

**103.** No. A player can only be dismissed by the referee.

**104.** No. The ball is out of play when it crosses the goal-line. A goal-kick is the correct decision.

**105.** No. Goalkeepers are allowed a maximum of 4 steps while holding, bouncing, or throwing the ball in the air. An indirect free-kick should be awarded.

**106.** No, if he is satisfied that the defender did not handle the ball intentionally.

**107.** No, because the goalkeeper did not strike the opponent intentionally.

**108.** A penalty, because the goalkeeper is holding the opponent.

**109.** If the objects cannot be made safe, the player must not be allowed to play.

**110.** A direct free-kick should be awarded, or a penalty-kick if the offender was inside his own penalty-area.

**111.** The ball must be dropped again. It is not in play until it touches the ground.

**112.** The offender must be dismissed and play restarted with a throw-in.

**113.** Not unless his shirt can be confused with any other player, but he should be advised to wear the shirt of the player he is replacing.

**114.** Yes. The defender may also be cautioned for leaving the field without permission.

**115.** The ball pressure must be 0.6 to 0.7 atmospheres (9.0 to 10.5 lb/sq.in.).

**116.** The goalkeeper should be cautioned for ungentlemanly conduct and an indirect free-kick awarded to the opposing team.

**117.** No. The player must be cautioned and an indirect free-kick awarded to the opposing team from where the player received the ball.

**118.** Yes, because the free-kick is outside the penalty-area and the attacker is more than 9.15 metres (10 yards) from the ball.

**119.** No. An indirect free-kick must be awarded against the corner-kicker for playing the ball twice before another player has touched it.

**120.** No. The attacker was in an off-side position, and clearly trying to gain an advantage, when the ball was kicked by his team-mate.

**121.** The player must be dismissed. By refusing to give his name he is committing another cautionable offence.

**122.** No. The ball had not crossed the goal-line. Play must be stopped and restarted by dropping the ball where it touched the helmet.

**123.** No. The coach may be reported for interfering with the game.

**124.** No. This is unfair obstruction. An indirect free-kick should be awarded against the attacking team.

**125.** Neither. There is no offence. The laws of the game do not require players to be numbered. If the competition requires numbered shirts, the matter can be reported after the match.

**126.** Yes. Any player of the attacking team may take the kick.

**127.** A goal-kick, because the ball was out of play; but the defender should be cautioned or dismissed.

**128.** The referee is the sole judge of playing conditions and his decision is final.

**129.** Yes. Both feet must be on the ground. The opposing team will be awarded a throw-in.

**130.** No. The goalkeeper may be charged inside the goal-area only if he is holding the ball or is obstructing an opponent. Indirect free-kick.

**131.** No. The corner-post must be replaced before the corner-kick is taken.

**132.** No. It is dangerous play. Indirect free-kick.

**133.** The defender must be cautioned and play restarted with another goal-kick because the ball was not in play when the offence occurred.

**134.** No, the correct decision is a corner-kick.

**135.** No. Obstruction is an indirect free-kick offence. A goal cannot be allowed. The correct decision is a goal-kick.

**136.** A penalty-kick is the correct decision.

**137.** No. The free-kick must be retaken because the ball did not pass outside the penalty-area into play.

**138.** The action of the opponent was unfair on the kicker: an indirect free-kick should be awarded against the offender's team.

**139.** Yes. The substitute may be cautioned. If play is stopped for the caution, it must be restarted with a dropped ball.

**140.** Yes. There is no restriction on where the attackers may stand.

**141.** Yes. But he must not attempt to obstruct the goalkeeper when the corner-kick is taken.

**142.** A penalty-kick, because the offence was initiated inside the penalty-area.

**143.** The players must be recalled for the remaining 2 minutes of the first half.

**144.** No. The law requires a throw-in to be taken with two hands. As a result, another player should take the throw-in.

**145.** Yes. Seven players are the minimum acceptable for the match to be valid.

**146.** None. Play should continue. The tackle was fair because the ball was played first.

**147.** No. The defender should be instructed to move away to avoid distracting the penalty-kicker.

**148.** The goal-kick must be retaken because it was not in play, i.e., it had not passed outside the penalty-area before it crossed the goal-line.

**149.** Yes, because the attacker did not handle the ball intentionally.

**150.** Yes, provided the ball is touched once only.

# Are you a SOCCER EXPERT?

Check your rating here.

Marking system:

(a)  For each completely correct answer award yourself 5 points.

(b)  For a partially correct answer grade your mark according to the degree of success, i.e., 1, 2, 3 or 4 points.

*Example:*  If your answer to Problem 16 is NO but you have not said that an indirect free-kick should be awarded — allow 3 points.

Add up all your points and check your degree of soccer knowledge with the following guide:

| MARKS | RATING |
|---|---|
| 750–650 | You are truly a SOCCER EXPERT. All referees should achieve totals within this range. |
| 650–550 | You have an excellent knowledge of soccer problems. All experienced players should score a minimum of 550. |
| 550–450 | A very good level, which should be achieved by keen fans and young players. |
| 450–300 | An average score, making good base for improvement. |
| 300 or less | You are probably content just to follow the flow of play. You will find more enjoyment with improved knowledge. |

If you want to improve your rating and achieve SOCCER EXPERT status, re-check the problems which proved difficult and find the correct answers. After two weeks test yourself again, answering all problems and compare your score. You will improve rapidly with this method.